Keep It Simple:

For Carers: A Light-hearted Guide to Dementia

First published in Great Britain in 2024 by Dr. A. Walker-Fraser

Copyright © Alison Walker-Fraser 2024
Email: xifra9@gmail.com

All rights reserved. No part of this publication can be reproduced, stored in a retrieval system, or transmitted, in any other form or by any means without the prior written permission, in any form, nor be otherwise circulated in any form of binding or cover other than that in which it is published and without a similar condition being imposed on the subsequent publisher.

Paperback ISBN: 978-1-7391131-5-5

Printed and Bound in Great Britain by Amazon.

Contents

	In a Nutshell	5
1	Relax, its only Uncertainty	13
2	The Expert	21
3	The Actor	29
4	The Vanishing Lady	35
5	Feeling Our Way Around	43
6	Storm Clouds	53
7	Twists and Turns	63
8	Carers need Care Too	71
9	Lost in Time	73
10	Time to Go	79
	Useful Resources	84

For Glenda and Amber who understand the challenges of caregiving

In a Nutshell

This is a hard one to crack.

Imagine feeling lost and confused in a world that was once familiar. Imagine struggling to make sense of the day to day things that previously were automated in your memory. Imagine not recognising your home, your family, your friends, yourself.

The World Health Organisation estimates there are 55 million people living with dementia worldwide. Every year, the figure increases by 10 million. In the UK, this is today's nightmare for one in 11 people over the age of 65 and for over 40,000 people below the age of 60.

There are many faces of dementia. Every person who develops some form of dementia – whether it be Alzheimer's, Vascular, Lewy Body, mixed dementia, frontotemporal – will have different and similar features that will manifest in the course of the disease.

Diagnosis of the type of dementia can usually be achieved through a variety of tests, which can be difficult and time-consuming to obtain. Certainly, it involves a specialist referral, which may include blood tests and MRI scans, to determine the patient's neurological, functional and behavioural capabilities. Persistence and patience are required in seeking a diagnosis.

At present, there is no solution to the crisis but for those in the mix, life becomes filled with experiences that range from the sublime to the ridiculous, from the incredulous to the accepting, both hilarious the quality of life and deliver compassionate care to those with dementia. Isn't that what we would all like, if we were the dementia sufferer?

This booklet is not a medical guide but a general one based on practical experience, designed to enlighten. Each chapter depicts the change. Each chapter suggests strategies to help.

Each chapter within this booklet contains some top tips for carers, interwoven with the story of Mary and her journey through the Alzheimer's Maze - real events, conversations and action using the fictional style of 'letters' between the key protagonists. The examples given are humorous, light hearted examples of what can happen in a person's journey with dementia.

Remember, there are common threads to the dementia journey but everyone's journey is individual.

Remember keep communication simple.

Respect and Care with love and humanity.

o   o   o   o   o   o   o   o   o   o

and awful. The journey through the dementia maze will be a huge learning experience, not just about dementia but about relationships, understandings and emotions.

What can you expect to see and hear?

The various forms of dementia will throw up different behaviours over time. But there are a number of common threads

- Confusions and disorientation – lost and 'spaced-out', even in familiar places or settings.
- Behavioural change - such as agitation, restlessness, wandering, anxiety, aggression, despair, depression, mood swings.
- Communication issues – unable to talk, read or write, to understand instructions, to follow or hold a conversation.
- Difficulties with daily tasks such as cooking, washing, dressing, problem solving, follow routines, mobility.
- Memory loss – unable to remember names, people, places, objects, time, repeating questions & answers, lack of special awareness.
- In the latter stages of the disease, the body begins to shut down and incontinence, swallowing, moving, become more difficult. The immune system weakens and infection becomes more common.

What are the strategies for the dementia sufferer in the absence of a cure?

Research has shown that social interaction helps those living with dementia; it improves well-being. Social isolation, on the other hand, is linked to an increased risk of dementia and an acceleration of the disease. Everyone who needs support and care is a whole human being, deserving of our time, love and interaction and not just to get them from A to B. Some of the therapies that can enrich the quality of life, includes –

- Non pharmacological therapies such as art, music, reminiscence, games & memory exercises.
- Increased socialisation, gentle exercise, healthy diet.
- Medication, as prescribed by health practitioners to help slow the progression of the disease and the treatment of specific behavioural symptoms. It is important to remember that drug therapy, tailored to the patient's specific issues and history, is prescribed only by a doctor taking into account the risks and advantages and, monitored regularly for side effects.

So, whether you are a professional carer or a family carer, how do you cope with this? How do you manage the emotional, physical and often financial stresses of caring? How do you help the sufferer live as comfortable and pleasant a life as possible?

One thing is for sure, this disease is not abating. There is no cure. Your skills and expertise are in demand. Globally, the numbers of people living with dementia is predicted to grow to around 139 million by 2050 (WHO). Despite almost **one million people** in the UK living with dementia today, and it being the UK's leading cause of death, there is still a widespread lack of awareness around the impact it has on people affected by the condition. Society isn't a particularly supportive or friendly place for those living with dementia, owing to a lack of practical support, and so people quickly become distressed.

This guide is written in a way that shares both tips and techniques in caring for someone, with whatever type of dementia, interspersed with stories from personal experience (written in the from of letters between Mary who suffered from Alzheimer's and her family of carers).

The disease throws life and everything that goes with it, out of balance. It is a journey of fundamental conflict between the expectation of living with the disease and the cruelty of reality. There are risks and dangers, there are highs and lows, there are moments of joy and despair. The purpose of this story, and guide, is a greater understanding for all engaged in caring.

For carers, having access to counselling, short term respite, a support network (including online dementia support groups) are vital to the personal carer. Good care training and support for the professional carer should be at the forefront of all commercial and public care homes.

While there will much laughter and some tears, it will be a harrowing journey. There will be despair, pain and loss, in different ways, for all involved. Death is part of living but the brain is our being, so to lose it denies us any humanity or control in the run up to death.

In the absence of any medical options for dementia suffers, it comes down to those who love and care for them to deliver a 'good life'. Anyone struggling, looking confused or lost, deserves our help and kindness, no matter how busy we are. The positivity we offer is to love and laugh with them and honour their memory. The unhappiness and grief we feel becomes our hidden secret in their presence.

The world of dementia is a theatre for the enactment of comedy, drama and tragedy. In moments of miscommunication and new developments, my advice is to embrace improvisation. You don't believe you have any acting skills? Well, it is time to learn, because it makes the caring journey so much easier.

Abandon any preference you may have for rational, logical and analytical thinking – this has no relevance in the world that we are about to enter. Of course, health and safety is the baseline but beyond that life is about happiness. Be their guide through the maze, rather than the expert that 'tells'. Listen, respect boundaries (whatever they might be) and get involved in their 'new' world.

From now on, it is '***feelings not facts***' that are the focus of the day. When you find the child within you, then the art of communication and collaboration becomes more readily available and the relationship between you will grow in a new direction; one that will serve you both, in the coming days and months.

Create new memories, albeit 'in the moment'. Find time for new experiences whether they be in the home or externally. Yes, you do need to 'risk assess' but apply a portion of common sense, in terms of how impactful it would be. Don't shut off new experiences because you are fearful of coping, but do cover all eventualities. There is no predictability in the dementia maze. Every day can be different..

To be a 'good' carer, you need to be focused on the 'other'. Learn and listen with your heart, in order to connect emotionally. Be **PERSON FOCUSED** not **disease focused.** Not only does it boost the quality of life for those with dementia, it helps make the carer's job more satisfying and an enriching experience. Remember there is more to the person that their disease.

Relationship. Relationship, Relationship is everything.
Be involved in their journey.
There is more to the person than dementia…

One day it might be you who needs that compassionate voice and interaction to get through the challenge of the day. All of us benefit from the gentle power of touch, of warmth, of comfort and support.

- Be kind and compassionate.
- Be animated and tender.
- Be involved in who the person was and has become.
- Be the one that makes a difference.

If you are a professional carer, be culturally sensitive and aware. For each individual in your care, will have a variety of cultural beliefs, values, experiences. Cultural preconceptions could result in poor care for the individual. Carers must be open-minded, non judgemental and willing to learn. In the care home, training on cultural variances, cultural behaviours and the modification of the environment needs to be taken into account. The person's cultural preference is critical to good, quality care.

Training and education in care giving is a must for all professional carers, Carers should be able to be flexible and adaptable. Modifying how they approach those in their care. Being self aware and culturally astute may affect how they engage with their 'clients'.

Caring for someone with dementia requires a multi-- dimension approach to their physical, social, emotional and cultural needs. By using a variety of tools and techniques, carers can improve

1.
Relax, its only Uncertainty

"Never be in a hurry; do everything quietly and in a calm spirit. Do not lose your inner peace for anything whatsoever, even if your whole world seems upset". *(Francis de Salles)*

1. **Recognise that everyone's journey through the dementia maze will be different. Each phase of the disease will bring a new set of surprises, challenges and a need to do things differently from before. There will be no status quo.**

2. **Be understanding and compassionate. Dementia dooms one to an eternal present and the cold medical facts can make a person despair. In the early stage, dementia blunts the sharp edges of reality, but for all the smiles, there is an absence.**

3. **Smile, relax and remember, this change in their life is 'new' to your loved one / client too (although they may not see it that way).**

4. **Frustrations, agitations, disquiets will surface. Remain calm. Smile, breathe, engage.**

5. Patience is a virtue that YOU need since you may not see it in them. Allow plenty of time when planning activities or routines. Do not rush them.

6. Become a best friend, a co-conspirator ... agree with their way of thinking. Mirror their comments
e.g. "I don't remember either.. what a pair we are ! "

7. If you are having a 'bad' day, try not to show it because they will read your facial and body expressions which can affect their response.

8. Do not correct. Otherwise you will become upset in turn and then there is a mountain to climb to restore calm. Divert. Talk. Hold their hand. Make them laugh. The black cloud will pass.

9. Activity – old and new – helps keep the focus and the engagement. Sitting doing nothing is the route to an early grave. Engage then in some activity, no matter how short.

10. Lucidity will come and go….crystal clear in speech and thought one minute/ one hour/ one day and then it's gone…sometimes to return, sometimes not. Learn to read the behaviours and communication, whether verbal or otherwise.

o o o o o o o o

Dear Neighbours

It is a terrible disease this dementia. I think I have known for some time that I have it but the doctor gave me confirmation, following scans and a psychiatric assessment. I am not mad, so seeing a clinical psychiatrist was something of a shock. Or maybe I am unhinged, for there are certain moments when I can do some really daft things ! Were you aware of the fact that I had lost the plot on occasions? Oh, you were... well, that is a surprise... I thought no-one noticed the change. Gosh, did I really do the following.?

On one occasion, when I put food into the microwave to heat, disaster struck. Those were the days when I could actually remember how to use a microwave ! Happy in the knowledge that all was well, I got on with other things around the house and promptly forgot all about the food. Still, there is no harm in heating food, right? Well, that is assuming one has the correct setting and timing to reheat, not full blast, for the maximum period possible. I decided to go out to the shops, for a few basic essentials; only a short trip for 40 minutes or so...

What a commotion on return...police, fire engine, and neighbours all busy in vicinity of my flat. Apparently the smell of burning and smoke had triggered a full scale emergency response. My front door had been broken to gain access in order to ascertain what was happening. I was somewhat shocked but calm, as I explained I had only been reheating food in the microwave. Turns out, it had been cooking at full temperature for an hour and then spontaneously combusted, resulting in smoke. Well, no harm done, then eh? The police lady was quite officious and frightened me more than the smoking microwave. A cup of tea would have been nice and maybe a sweet biscuit for the shock...

I was always quite a good cook and loved to make oatcakes. Did you try them at any stage? Yes, when you came to play scrabble with me on a weekly basis. Oh, did we do that? I couldn't play it now that's for sure...no words come these days.

I came to yours for coffee on a number of occasions? Really and where do you live? Oh, well if you say so, then it must be correct...You were concerned that I was often to be seen at my door calling out "who is there"? Well, you never can be too careful who comes and goes in an apartment block with no concierge. Was that my role ?!

Yes, I remember the gardener who tended to the communal gardens at the apartment block. Charming, young man and so helpful, in cutting the grass and tidying the flower borders, that I decided to reward him handsomely. I was unsure as to the cost, so suggested that he take from my purse whatever was appropriate. Not sure why that should send him into something of a panic; so much so, he reported it to the chair of the apartments committee.

Oh, it was already paid for by our annual service charge? Well, that was news to me...

Ah, Misty, my darling little Westie, what a lovely dog she was. Bit of a pest at times but a loyal companion nonetheless. She had become something of a nuisance always needing to be taken out for walk. There were times when I decided she didn't need to go
out. But then she would relieve herself in the house...naughty dog. Yes, she did go missing one evening and I had no idea where she was but I wasn't too concerned, particularly when she was on my doorstep the following morning, ready for her breakfast.

Apparently, she had been shut in the apartment block's stairwell all night, for she left evidence of her presence. I do not know how that could have happened...

Dogs are funny things. They keep you amused but they are a terrible tie, preventing you from doing what you might want to do. The amount of time that I have spent looking for the animals, in the flat and in the town, doesn't bear thinking about...what a waste of my time. Trailing the streets looking for the other dog, asking people if they had seen her and returning home empty handed. Did I tell you that I had two dogs and a cat? I did but you only ever saw one dog in the ten years that I lived at the flat? So, dogs plural is a mystery, as is the cat? Ah well, you were just unlucky because they were there...I think…some of the time…possibly…who knows.

It was always tricky remembering when people were coming to visit. Fortunately, I lived close to a railway station so it was easy for my visitors to travel to me. I rarely travelled by train, so had no reason to use the station. What was that? I was often to be found standing on the platform in the evening waiting for my visitors to arrive. What visitors were those? You don't know and neither did I?

Well...I don't remember who came on the train that particular evening but I am sure it was lovely to see them evening but I am sure it was lovely to see them. My daughter tells me that I telephoned her on one occasion to ask where she was since I had been waiting for hours at the station and she was at home in England. Another time, she arrived by train, to be told by me that while it was great to see her, I was waiting on someone arriving and have time to chat...

Mad, or what, eh!

I was a regular member of the women's guild and enjoyed the monthly talks and outings. It was marvellous that it was only a short walk from the flat to the church hall. I did enjoy walking although I was happy to take a lift, if one was offered. I scared you on one particular evening, at the close of the meeting, by announcing that I had a lift arranged with my husband who would be waiting outside in the car. Sorry, about that ... I didn't even know that I had been married. Oh, he has been dead ten years or more. Ah, I take your point. Funny thing this memory loss...

I do know - I think – that I have had some wonderful holidays with the family in recent years. All of which were great fun. Ah, you tell me that I could be difficult when a slight degree of petulance crept in at not being able to do what I wanted !

Mmn, not sure about that. More likely I knew exactly where and what I wanted to do and will have gone off alone, on a mission to undertake whatever came into my mind at the time. Family can be irksome when they lose track of time and wonder where you have been. Fear not, I am in control of my actions, if not always my mind!

You tell me that I am lucky to have a loving daughter to take care of me. Yes, absolutely...erm, who is that? Does she know that she is my daughter? Oh hang on a minute, I remember now. Yes, this is indeed my eldest daughter. I sold my car to my grandson for £1, although that is disputed by the family. But he did get a good little 'run around' for a very fair price. The family were concerned that I might drive off and forget where I was. Really, as if I would !

So, dear friends, I cannot stop too long because I have decided that the best solution is to go live with my daughter.

I am crystal clear in my mind. It is the right thing, the only thing, to do since I know this disease will only get worse and I will not cope alone. I do not want to go into a home. I will be sad to leave but it is for the best. I know it is for the best and my friends and neighbours agree. Sometimes, life can be very unexpected but you just have to adapt and get on with it.

So this is a short visit to say,
 'adios, amigos'.

Love, Mary

2. The Expert

*"Before you are wise, After you are wise,
In between you are otherwise"* (David Zindell)

- **The 'expert knows best' is a theme that becomes more relevant as the dementia progresses. As conversational skills diminished, it is important that the dementia sufferer retains a sense of control. Promoting independence, by letting them do as much as they can (even if it takes time) helps encourage a sense of freedom and self-worth. Establishing daily routines helps provide structure, stability and eases disorientation. But be flexible in the routines as the behaviours change over time.**

1. **Simplify tasks to reduce their sense of overload. Use visual clues to help them remember what to do.** *e.g. if they have enjoyed house cleaning, leave the floor brush visible (but in a safe place!)*
2. **Don't ask direct questions. Don't contradict - no matter what, for s/he is the expert.**
   Agreement on what the 'expert' thinks, retains a sense of value for the person.

3. **Detail can be unhelpful and confusing. Operate on a 'need to know' basis, in the moment rather than the long term. Bite-size chunks. Drip feed the thought process** *e.g. " You were probably thinking the same as I was…that this is the shop we use"*

4. **Advocacy not questioning. Make suggestions, share your thinking (positive only) and manoeuvre through appreciative comments.** *e.g. "I wondered whether we might make another visit sometime soon (conspiracy - advocacy)"* **rather than telling s/he they have an appointment next week (when time and space are unconnected in the memory).**

5. **Explanations were best offered in the form of** *"What works for me, may work for you, how about we do X."*.

6. **Ask for their help, with the accompanying remark that they are better in the activity than the instigator of the request.**

7. **Transference is a wonderful behaviour that can be managed with care and forethought.** *For example, wandering aimlessly with a blank and confused expression could be alleviated by you, the carer, beaming smiles, laughing, singing and dancing.*

8. **Concentrate on feelings not facts and give positive reinforcement.** *For example,*
"You are so good at washing up. Thank you for turning on the warm water to wash the dishes. "

9. **Offer eye contact at all times. Smile, smile, smile.**

10. **Tackling repetition with repetition changes the game plan. Repetition, if left unchecked can be an irritation to the listener and a trigger for increased anxiety by the person with dementia.**
    ◦ Focus on the emotion not the behaviour – rather then react, think about what s/he is feeling.

    ◦ Give the person the answer that s/he is looking for, even if you have to repeat it several times.

    ◦ Use memory aids. If the person asks the same questions over and over again, offer reminders by using notes, clocks, or photographs, if these items are still meaningful.

    ◦ Accept the behaviour, and work with it. If it isn't harmful, don't worry about it.

    ◦ Turn the action/behaviour into an activity. Engage the person in an activity. The individual may simply be bored and need something to do.

- Communicate in simple, plain language, speak slowly & clearly, no long sentences, visual aids to help, positive body language, minimise distraction when speaking, show respect and empathy.
- Be patient.

o o o o o o o o o

Dear Speech Therapist

I have been told that it is important to read aloud and practice my speech: use it or lose it. Well, I am trying – in more ways than one, apparently – yet, there are occasions when I am insulted by the efforts of others. To be given Jack and Jill type books, by you, a speech & language specialist, is not my idea of fun. Call yourself an expert ! Clearly, a charlatan if that's all you can offer me to read. I would rather have used a copy of the Saga magazine. I can assure you, there are better ways to practice. I should know, I am the expert.

It is a bit tricky following conversations with others. They always say too much and I get lost. Can we keep it simple, please? And of course, when I start to look confused by their efforts, then I get that look from them, so I just give up. There are times when others seem to be at cross-purposes with my line of thinking and conversation, which makes it amusing, if not incomprehensible.

Television is a wonderful reading source, is it not? I love to sit and read aloud from the subtitles. It can be a struggle when some of the translation results in unknown words. On and on I go...it is great...though maybe not so great for others watching TV with me. Their choice is either to be deafened by the volume or my reading aloud ! Sometimes the speech moves rather too quickly for me but I try to persevere for the length of the programme. I tell others, not to worry... I am just speaking to myself...in case they think I have lost the plot!

Monologues have always been a successful form of entertainment. I take my inspiration from the likes of Joyce Grenfell and Eve Ensler, and from the telephone conversations I listen to, especially when my daughter is chatting to friends.

For example, last night was such good fun as we laughed together for over an hour. I have no idea who she was speaking to but I was happy to contribute to the conversation. Three of us in the same room conversing in a two-way manner on the phone. Clever, eh !

Was I invited to participate ? No, but what does that matter, I had a great time chatting to someone.

Alison laughed and gestured that she was on the telephone, waving at the handset, stuck to her ear. I think she wanted me to speak to her at the same time as she spoke to her friend... happy to oblige.

Holidays, you said? You are not planning any? Funny that you should mention that - I am planning a holiday. It will be a grand affair since I am thinking of going back to that place, from where I have just returned.

Sorry, you lost me there ? Something about it being a bit of an adjustment? Well, I can adjust the size - possibly drop a dress size for my holiday. She's pointing the phone again – maybe I should talk more loudly, if she cannot hear me?

She is waving again and moving into the next room.

Hang on, I am coming too.

Well, as I was saying...yada, yada, yada. Oops, are you keeping up with me ?

Of course, I shall not be staying with those people this time, when we go on holiday... terrible house, horrible people. Now, I suggest you come too and we will travel together.

Good, I can arrange it.

What was that you said about equations? I guess there are no points to equate to. Ah, I heard you mention cash ... okay, I am going to going to check if the cash is there.

Heavens, it's complicated running a three-way conversation, especially when I was not on the phone. But a good laugh all the same. And of course, I was practising my speech !

Speaking of practising my speech. I had lunch today at the Alzheimer's society. What poor souls some of them are. They just cannot talk properly....heaven knows, what the man sitting next to me was talking about. So, the best thing to do is ignore it and run your own conversation but direct it at him. I just laugh, smile, hold their hands and twitter. It works wonders for me. It is a shame when the person cannot follow your conversation but at least I know that I am doing them some good.

Alison has bought some sort of computer game on brain training. I wonder if she feels her brain is not as good as it ought to be, since she spends a lot of time sharing this activity with me. I do not like the man on the machine... he sounds very strange. Anyway, to keep her happy, I speak aloud to the machine but it is pretty boring, I can tell you. It seems to consist of calling out colours and numbers. I really don't see the point of it. I might as well go back to the Jack and Jill books.

What is the saying...quality not quantity? Well, let me tell you ... reading the newspaper is a heck of a lot of quantity. Every morning, The Telegraph newspaper is placed in front of me and I am encouraged to read aloud. Yes, the headlines are easy and quite interesting...the cartoons are fun...but I could be dead long before I get to the fashion tips! And it would be a shame to miss this section since I am a great follower of fashion and a creative designer myself. I do wonder whether all this reading aloud is worthwhile. Perhaps, the others should spend their time practising?

I should mention though, I am dedicated to my own self-development and have risen from my bed.

What time is it, I wonder? Oh, it is midnight. Time to continue reading the newspaper aloud.

So, I managed to get another hour's practice in.

Sweet dreams, everyone...

Love Mary

3. The Actor

> *"There is in every child at every stage a new miracle of vigorous unfolding, which constitutes a new hope and a new responsibility for all. "* (Erik Erikson)

1. Acting involves a broad range of skills, including a well-developed imagination, emotional facility, physical expression, vocal projection, clarity of speech and, the ability to interpret drama.
Develop this love for acting, for it will serve you well in caring for the dementia sufferer.

2. Reason has no part to play in the dementia world. It is not about making sense in your world, but from theirs. They do not have the ability to reason.

3. As the brain changes, skills and capabilities become limited. Reframe your expectations and behaviours, for they will not be able to do so.

4. Join in the game play. Act. Be on their level. Most plays have drama, laughter, tears, suspense, mystery, surprise. All of which you will see in the course of time.

5. Communication needs to be kept brief and positive. Too much detail and they will become more confused. Repetition is the name of the game.

6. Do not argue, disagree, or raise your voice. Play the role to connect with them. Distract if need be.

7. Do not correct. You are a player in their world, go with the flow. Encourage them to play, act and find some joy. Be the adult but with respect for the needs of a child.

8. The environment needs to be friendly, functional, familiar and supportive.

9. You may not recognise who they appear to have become, in terms of behaviours. Personality traits may change/ materialise. Remember who the person is - heart and soul – not who they become.

10. Fondness and forgiveness are the responsibilities we have, in supporting them.

o o o o o o o o o

Dear Actor

It's official. We are going to have some fun today. Whoopee !

I am in a playful mood so let's get out of here. I have just checked the gate and found that someone has not applied enough tension to the cycle lock that secures the garden, so we can wriggle through. I have done it before so just follow me. The Great Escape here we go...

What do you want to do, first? How about skipping along the lane – we won't need any skipping ropes, just extend your arms like an aeroplane, rock from side to side and skip. Look and learn from the expert, I try to do this each day when walking the dogs. Whew, its' pretty exhausting, I don't think I can go too far doing that! Maybe, power walking would get us further, faster and burn off the calories with our wiggling. Swing those hips, girls...

Isn't this fun! I love the freedom of not being told what to do all the time. Adults are a pretty boring lot, with their rules and regulations and 'I know best' attitude. I just pull faces at them when they start to go on and on and on.....It really annoys them, so I do it some more! And I am really, really good at acting. Maybe I should have been an actor. Watch this...

Here I am playing dead. If you don't want to do anything they say, just collapse in the chair or the bed or the floor and feign unconsciousness. Try to keep it going for as long as possible, so that they become unsure as to whether it is real or play-acting. I can go a whole 5 minutes – well, it seems that long.

Or another trick is playing blind, deaf and dumb. It's a sure winner! When they ask you a question, don't speak. Mime that you cannot understand what is being asked of you. Communicate with them using sign language. Top performance is to combine it with feigning unconsciousness!

One of my best performances was fluttering my eyelashes, rolling my eyes, staggering upstairs and collapsing with moans and groans along the way. Keep your eyes firmly shut when they are looking at you. As a finale, I wait several minutes at the end before opening my eyes, exclaiming I don't know what is happening and suggesting some chocolate might be of help. Where's my Oscar?

I have heard somewhere that laughter is the best medicine. So, I am practicing a range of laughs to use in different circumstance, some of which are irritating to adults. There is the shrill 'ha, ha, ha' laugh to be used as an accompaniment to the statement ' I really don't think so'. This gets the message across that I am not amused.

There is a good, hearty laugh for any programme that you watch on TV, whether funny or not and the 'he, he, he' laugh which is exclusive to me (no explanation to others, since it is my personal joke). But I am willing to share laughter and sometimes it is good to laugh together, although I am not always sure why we are laughing - still, no matter, it is all fun!

Listen, why don't we have our own secret language? Then we could share without others knowing what we are talking about! Let's make up words and jumble up our sentences. As long as we know what we mean, then it doesn't really matter that we cannot be understood by adults.

I am getting better at doing this, these days – so much so,

that sometimes, even I don't know what I mean! Stupid or what... Whispering Island would be a great place to be, where all day long we would talk in hushed tones, using our own secret code.

I am also practicing Queen's English though, with particular emphasis on intonation for greatest impact. Don't you find some adults are far too nosey, wanting to know all your business, or asking impertinent questions of a personal nature?

Haughty, is a useful tone to use when accompanied by phrases such as, 'I beg your pardon', 'I am not amused, 'Really? I think not' and 'how dare you'. My expression of disdain, when pronouncing such phrases, has some notoriety in family circles. Well, it is important to let others know I am the expert.

Apparently, 75% of communication is non-verbal language. Well, I knew that just by looking at your face. Grim. Don't smile or your face might crack ...

I love rolling my eyes when I am being told what I must or must not do. My best response is to stick out my tongue, then laugh. I read faces. I spend a lot of time watching and if I don't get a reaction, I just keep staring. I gather it can be rather off putting to some people. What fun it is to be a nuisance and an irritant !

The important thing is to act out a variety of roles and just enjoy the reactions. I am a budding, Oscar winning actor.

Love Mary, aged 13¾

4.
The Vanishing Lady

"If I had a world of my own, everything would be nonsense. Nothing would be what it is, because everything would be what it isn't. And contrary wise, what is, it wouldn't be. And what it wouldn't be, it would. You see?" (Lewis Carroll)

- **While still mobile, trips outdoors provide stimulus, fresh air and the 'feel good' factor. Of course, ensuring safety is a priority to avoid any mishaps. Keeping a close eye on them, is an obvious need. Choosing the best time of day when they will be alert and complaint (hopefully), taking account of weather and temperatures. Choosing quiet, safe and familiar locations. Paying attention to suitable footwear and clothing Behaviours can change in the course of any outing, so a contingency plan ready.**

1. **Wandering and restlessness are common features, of the disease. Accept it and ensure that the environment is a safe place as they go 'on their travels'.**

2. **Agree and reassure. Repeatedly, in an anxious state, there may be comments such as,** *Are we going now? 'Let's go'.* **Have fun, share in their fantasy.**

3. Disappearing is a common occurrence and if at home, it might be best to consider changing locks, adding garden gate locks to prevent them going out, day or night.

4. The police have considerable experience of looking for lost persons who suffer from dementia and, they recognise the need for addressing *'feelings not facts'* when finding them. When found, smile, laugh, hug, tell them how wonderful it is to see them again, suggest a cup of tea or whatever... Do not reprimand or comment on the disappearance. It's gone. Move on.

5. The name of the game is comfort, love, laughter and repetition. Every hour/ day/ week becomes a new one for them, so expect to have to listen and repeat again and again….

6. Bags packed, coat on, "off to visit person x" may be a regular occurrence at some stage. Become a **co-conspirator e.g."** *The taxi is coming but running late; the telephone call from x postponing the visit until tomorrow"*...**Dramatization to distract and deter.**

7. Share your experiences, tell or show them something interesting. Keep it short since their

ability to concentration is limited.

8. Crying, fear, agitation are real. A bad dream is a reality to them. No matter how often it happens and how busy you are, take a moment to wipe the tears away. Find something to distract...

9. Truculence, bad temper, bad behaviour will surface and often at times when you have little time for it. Overstimulation, tiredness can be triggers. Take a deep breadth, smile, try to deflect . If appropriate walk away and come back a short time later. By then, the dark clouds might have parted and the sun shines through.

10. Mood swings are common, resulting in liking and disliking people, refusing to participate one minute, then rushing headlong with excitement at the next. One minute, they are with you and the next lost in the maze. Calmy accept its part of the disease.

11. Research has shown that music therapy is an effective intervention to reduce behavioural symptoms – particularly aggression and anxiety, Make a playlist of songs they enjoy (Advice and resources are available on www.playlistforlife.org.uk)

o o o o o o o o o

Dear Friend

So, you are Mary, too? Fancy that…we have the same name. Well, dear friend, I am just going to the toilet – if I can find it (ha, ha) - so I will have a chat on the way back. We must be quiet though because everyone else is asleep.

Do you like living here? Have you seen my room? Why don't you come in? No-one need know. Back in a minute…

Hello again. Are you coming in? Oh well, maybe later then? I am not sure of the time but I am wondering whether to get dressed and go out. What do you think? Do you fancy coming with me?

Shh… better whisper so no one can hear us. I have just been into my room and checked. There would be room for you here. Why don't you come in and sleep here? It would be nice to talk more.

Oh look, here comes Alison. Have you met her?

Apparently, I have woken her with all my chatter to you, dear friend, who lives in the hallway mirror. Alison tells me its 2am and I should go back to bed. Well, I had better get going but not to bed. I am just about to go out. She is telling me to lower my voice, in case I wake others with all my chatter. I am not going back to bed. I don't care if anyone can hear me. I am talking to my friend.

Hello, dear friend. Are you still there? Good.

This is a terrible place; the sooner I am gone from here the better. You can't do anything around here.

What's your place like? Can I come to you?

I cannot seem to be able to get in. Where is the opening? Where? How? Damn, it is a struggle…

I don't understand what Alison is telling me. She says, it is a mirror and to stop pulling in case it comes off the wall. I explain that my friend is here and waiting for me and that I am going with her. I am trying to reach her. Alison tells me to go to bed which is what she is going to do now.

I wish to be left alone for I have a lot to do, sorting out my clothes, opening drawers, looking in wardrobes, opening and closing doors, checking that you are still there.

Are you there? Ah, good you are still watching.

Did I leave something in the bathroom? Better check the bathroom. Oops, wrong room. What does this say on the door? 'Alison and Allan's room.'

"Hello, are you asleep? Are you unwell? Why are you in bed? Why are you whispering?"

No, I am not going to bed. Ridiculous! I have a lot to do… Look at the time. Yes, 3am… I know the time, which is why I need to get on.

Endless, do this, do that, you cannot do this….What a place. Okay, I will sit down in the armchair but I am NOT going to bed.

Bye, bye… you go back to bed, then.

Hello again, dear friend.. I thought you had vanished.!

Do you fancy coming downstairs with me? Come on, I am feeling rather peckish.

Have you met the dogs? Come on doggies, time for a walk.

Where is the light switch? I wonder if it is this illuminated panel? Well, something happened because it is making a noise now, yet the light has not come on.

Drat, I cannot get the door open to let the dogs out...

Do you want something to eat? There is never anything to eat here... I am always starving! Ah, bread... that's good. Cereal, porridge, juice, all together in a bowl. Marvellous!

I will have a seat on the sofa and eat it there. It is getting very warm in here...

Oh, hello, it is Alison again. What time is it?

What is this wetness, you ask. Oh, someone has spilled food. No, I do not know who made this mess.

Is it time for bed, I wonder?. It is 8 am, you say. Is that bedtime? Stand-up? I don't understand, what you want me to do. I am happy to stay here. It is lovely and warm.

What was that you said about heating on all night? I really don't know anything about it. A mystery, I am sure.

Alison does not seem to know what I am talking about when I ask about my friend.. Sometimes she can be incredibly dense. She does not seem to know all of my friends nor what has happened to those people who were here earlier..

I must go back upstairs to my room to dress but apparently not until I have had some breakfast. I do like to eat and porridge is a joy, but for now, I need to have a sleep, as my eyes are heavy.

I have been told to go upstairs and get dressed because its daytime...But I am ready.

I am always ready.

I have already got my trousers and fleece on, over my nightclothes and under my dressing gown. So, I am dressed. Always prepared…

A cuppa would be nice. Where is my breakfast?…

Love Mary

5. Feeling our way around the Maze

*"When you are listening to somebody, completely, attentively
Then you are listening not only to the words,
But also to the feelings of what's being conveyed
To the whole of it, not part of it. "* (anonymous)

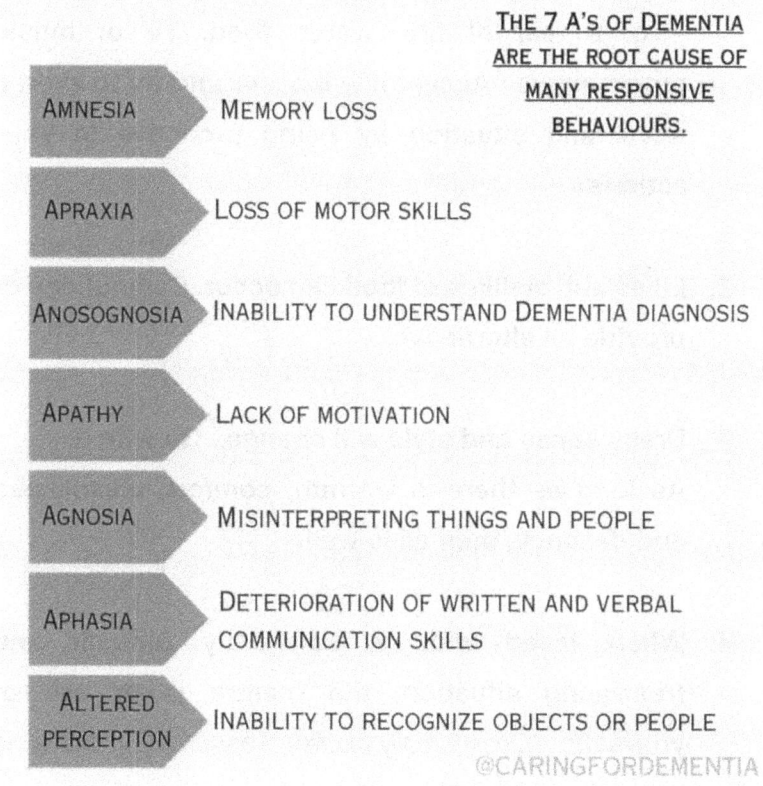

THE 7 A'S OF DEMENTIA ARE THE ROOT CAUSE OF MANY RESPONSIVE BEHAVIOURS.

- AMNESIA — MEMORY LOSS
- APRAXIA — LOSS OF MOTOR SKILLS
- ANOSOGNOSIA — INABILITY TO UNDERSTAND DEMENTIA DIAGNOSIS
- APATHY — LACK OF MOTIVATION
- AGNOSIA — MISINTERPRETING THINGS AND PEOPLE
- APHASIA — DETERIORATION OF WRITTEN AND VERBAL COMMUNICATION SKILLS
- ALTERED PERCEPTION — INABILITY TO RECOGNIZE OBJECTS OR PEOPLE

@CARINGFORDEMENTIA

While there is common ground on the behaviours that arise from the different types of dementia, the pace of change is very individual. The 7 A's of dementia are often present in all, at some stage.

There is no rule book on how to handle caring in the dementia landscape. But some key tips, on feeling your way through this maze, includes -

1. Aversions can develop which did not exist before. —e.g. a fear of fire, water, food, TV or music programmes   Accept it will occur and try to avert a worsening situation by being proactive in your actions.

2. Likes and dislikes of food can occur. Camouflage or provide an alternative.

3. Dress sense and style will change. Go with it.
   As long as there is warmth, comfort, cleanliness and decency, then all is well.

4. When faced with a potentially difficult and frustrating situation, the mantra is to ask of **yourself:** *"Does it really matter?"* (assuming there is no health & safety risk).

5. Who's who ? Forgetting a name, a connection, a person is common. You know the individual; they know you as a 'friend', so that all that matters. Make the bond and keep the relationship going.

6. NEVER ask them if they remember someone or something. Better for you to say *"I remember when"* Make a statement don't invite a memory or comment. If it triggers a memory, it will come. If not, so be it.

7. 'Sundowning' is a common, end of day, occurrence, when agitation and distress can increase.
Never bring up topics that might upset them.
    - Use distraction techniques: go into a different room, make the person a drink, have a snack, turn some music on, or go out for a walk (if possible).
    - Ask them what the matter is. Listen carefully to their response and if possible, see if you can deal with the reason for their distress .
    - Talk in a slow, soothing way.
    - Speak in short sentences and give simple instructions to try to avoid confusion.
    - Hold the person's hand or sit close by them (at the side not in front) and stroke their arm.

8. Try to keep television or radio stations set to something calming and quiet. Sudden loud noises, can be distressing for a person with dementia .
9. Socialisation is important. Fostering social grouping, encouraging friends and family to visit, social events with others with dementia – these all help improve the quality of life for those with dementia.

o o o o o o o o o

Dear Vivienne Westwood

I read somewhere, you once said that fashion is "life-enhancing and, like everything that gives pleasure, it is worth doing well". Well, Mary would endorse this statement.

She now has a passionate interest in creative ensembles and of resurrecting old clothes for more modern appeal. Mary takes an inordinate amount of time and effort with her creations and is fully absorbed in the pleasure.

There are no rules or etiquette to follow, free form is the order of the day: She certainly does not want to look like everyone else. She has her own unique style. For example, this evening she has taken inspiration from Mrs. Overall (Victoria Wood's Acorn Antiques) with an ensemble that consists of a beautiful white and peppermint headscarf, turquoise polo-neck jumper worn as a body wrap, aquamarine fleece draped over shoulders, sage green apron and a collection of necklaces dangling from wrists and arms. The hearing aid is worn as an extension to an earring. Surprisingly, the colour combinations of each item are beautifully complementary.

Miss Sartorial Elegance has found her niche in night-to-day wear. I think Galliano, would admire her technique of wearing a bra on top of the nightdress. The adornment of the pink bed-jacket on top of the raspberry nightdress and white bra, purple skirt and moccasin slipper-shoes, all serves to link the bed-to-breakfast attire. White pearl necklace and blue glass beads add sparkle and tie-in the colour combination with the powder blue, dressing gown.

Guests at the dining table will feel somewhat underdressed in their cargo pants and Gap tops, when Miss Sartorial Elegance arrives for brunch (that's the earliest she will make an appearance). The fashion show continues with a mid-afternoon return to the wardrobe. One outfit per day is insufficient. She likes to ring the changes and be fully occupied.

Warmth is a high priority for Mary, so she has a penchant for double trousers with skirt on top. Pretty blouses in shades of pink are chosen, one after the other is layered on top: three being the preferred number for both tops and necklaces.

I am not sure about her attempt to wear a polo-neck as leg warmers. She manages to get her legs through the arms of the sweater and pull it up to the groin. It doesn't look too comfortable and mobility is compromised. The icing on the cake is the red angora hat, for both indoor and outdoor wear.

Throughout the selection and decision-making process, a running commentary can be heard, as Mary consults her alter ego. Despite many invitations, she is a little disappointed that her friend in the looking glass cannot join her on the catwalk.

With the central heating on full blast throughout day and evening, Mary has determined that it really is too warm now, so a reduction in clothing is required.

Hemlines are rising and the recurring statement is to dispense with any item of clothing deemed old fashioned. The mini-dress is once again in fashion, with the 80 year-old brigade. The raspberry nightdress has been resurrected and is now worn with 60-denier tights, shoes and cotton polo-neck jumper.

Headwear this evening consist of a pair of white knickers - clean ones, I hasten to add, in case you are wondering - worn in a way to resemble a bandana. Actually, it doesn't look too bad, although it took a few minutes to realise what it was. She is nothing if not inventive. If Zandra Rhodes can influence society's expectations for "ageless" dressing, then so too can Mary!

By mid evening, as a prelude to her intended departure to visit friends or the shops or her 'home', her choice this evening is polo neck sweater, camisole on top of sweater, corduroy trousers, raincoat and snood.

As for bed-wear – well, there really is no need to differentiate between day and evening attire – simply remove a number of layers and there you are! Miss Sartorial Elegance has an outfit ready for every occasion, real or imaginary...

I wonder how long this phase will last? It certainly keeps her fully occupied throughout the day.

It does bring a smile, and tears to my eyes, as we laugh together over her choice of fashion..

Regards, Alison

Dear Debs

So sorry, there is no hot water again. Mary left the tap running and has drained the hot water tank. She also left a towel in the sink so, we have actually had a flood, at the same time as a loss of hot water.

I agree, she has adopted a territorial approach to the bathroom but I didn't realise, until I heard your cries of help, that she was holding the bathroom door closed to prevent you getting out of the bathroom, until I heard your cries for help! But, thank you for making her laugh – she found the whole episode highly amusing - I heard her chuckling for ages thereafter.

If it is any consolation, you are not the first person that she has imprisoned in the bathroom. I agree, it is amazing that she has the strength to be able to resist the pull of the person inside the bathroom, as they fight to escape having failed to negotiate terms of release.

The irony is, that she herself is a very reluctant user of the bathroom and would no doubt identify, if she could, with the desire for escape. Getting her to shower or bathe is a herculean task and one I fear, we have not conquered. The face of failure is far too familiar. Hundreds of gallons of water have been wasted, owing to a refusal at the final hurdle. Hours have been spent trying to cajole Mary into the bath. The bathroom has resembled a sauna cubicle, in a bid to convince her it was not too cold to strip off. Requests to be left to get on with it herself, have occasionally resulted in success
and thus each time she convinces me to leave, I am optimistic.

Yet more often than not, my hopes are dashed and my frustration rises, as the bathing belle attempts to wash with nightdress on...and she wonders why she is both cold and wet? Anyone passing the bathroom during these escapades could be forgiven for thinking that a murder was taking place, as voices rise and Mary bangs around in sheer frustration and temper. Perhaps there is a plot here for Midsomer Murders!

Were you too warm last night? Yes? Mary had been playing with the central heating programmer once again, and the heating was on all night. It's bad enough living in a hothouse during the day, without having to endure it at night. Actually, this is our second water-heating programmer since she was so fascinated by the lights and buttons that she damaged the previous one.

I know, I thought too that it would have been more robust but Mary's determination to tamper is legendary! Lights, sockets, timers, programmers are all a source of fascination.

I am not sure what happened at the dinner table tonight but she certainly reacted furiously to your chat and laughter. Don't take it personally. I suspect she felt excluded in someway and that her voice was not heard. She has difficulty following a conversation and needs a simple invitation to contribute at intervals throughout the meal.

Yes, she does take on a whole new character when she is offended. I thought she was going play the drama queen and throw her wine over you, at one stage. As it was, she simply responded by adopting a feigned sigh of exasperation, accompanied by such comments as "really, I think not" and "I am not amused". She then ignored you when you spoke ! Most of the time, she is utterly charming and endearing. By tomorrow, she will have forgotten all about it.

No, don't worry, that stain on the carpet was there before you arrived. The new carpet is no longer new, given the difficulty in preventing Mary from going upstairs with dirty shoes, food, drink or using inappropriate cleaning products. It's an on-going challenge to prevent breakages, loss or damage.

It is best to adopt a philosophical attitude and accept that you cannot maintain show-house standards. Still, it would be nice to enjoy the experience of a new item for a little longer than we currently seem to do ! We can but dream..

Incidentally, do these knickers, jumper and bottle of shampoo belong to you? Ah, I thought so... found them in Mary's room.

Don't suppose the half-eaten banana that the knickers are wrapped around, is yours?

Thought not !

Thanks for being so understanding, A

6.
Storm Clouds

"Step by step, we make our way" *(Kate Mosse, Labyrinth)*

- A lack of stimulus, limited activities, weeks of snow and ice, can become contributory factors to a change in behaviour.

- Tiredness, lack of stimulus, illness and disagreement, a bad dream, too much sleep, too little sleep, a non-associated article in a magazine can unsettle the dementia sufferer.

- Time had no meaning. Day becomes night and night becomes day.

- Restlessness can be a common feature and take various forms, such as wringing their hands, pulling at their clothes, touching themselves inappropriately.

- Suspicion is a feature of the disease's journey. A person with dementia may become suspicious of those around them, even accusing others of theft, infidelity or other improper behaviour. While accusations can be hurtful, remember that the disease is causing these behaviours and try not to take offense.

- Depending on the type of dementia, hallucinations may be present. Assessing the risk is important and, in severe cases, may require medical intervention. However, often it may not require any intervention other than reassuring words and a gentle touch.

- Reading body language, in particular facial expressions, becomes a growing feature of the disease when the person is losing their communication skills. (Men with beards can be a problem because it is difficult to read the face).

- Taking a dislike to people, albeit temporary, can arise. Sometimes an individual can unintentionally offend through an incorrect facial expression, a wrong word or a failure to flatter.

- An aggressive state of biting, slapping, kicking, can materialise, with a refusal to cooperate. It is a phase that will pass with time and is best handled with a calm 'no' and diversion.

- Dementia scuppers any plans of order and timetabling, but trying to create a routine can be useful for all.

- Conversations, become increasing difficult to translate into anything intelligible for others. Knowing the person, helps in the translation as reading the body language becomes ever important.

- Quiet, contented moments are a treasured creation of time together. A fleeting glimpse of the true person creates a euphoria of pleasure, which, no matter how short, is a welcome return.

----

1. As the disease takes hold, frailties increase and cognitive abilities decrease. It goes without saying, that a risk assessment of the home/ room is crucial to maintain their safety. Modifying the living environment helps keep them safe and secure with quality of living. Actions include –
    ◦ Labelling items
    ◦ Minimising clutter

- Locking hazardous and danger items away
- Installing safety devises (non-slip rugs, grab rails, gate barrier)
- Good lighting
- Comfortable furniture & furnishings,
- Familiar items in sight and touch

2. By running a conversation alongside theirs, you might just be lucky and give the appropriate comfort, even though you don't think what you say is connected.

3. Learning to recognise the triggers of agitation, comes with experience. Knowing how to return to a contented state, requires patience, persuasion, parenting and good acting skills.

4. In situation of suspicion:
   - Don't take offence or argue or try to convince.
   - Listen, be reassuring, let the person know you care.
   - Offer a simple answer. Share your thoughts with the individual, but keep it simple.
   - Switch the focus to another activity. Engage the individual in an activity, or ask for help with a chore.

- ○ **Provide a comforting line to calm them if agitated** *e.g. I have spoke to X who had found it/ replace it tomorrow.* **In all likelihood, they issue will be forgotten. But repetition may be needed.**

5. **Being open to new possibilities, doing activities together and separately could still hold an enjoyable outcome for all. It's all about feelings.**
   For example, finding time to do a hand massage on a regular basis.

6. **Try not to interrupt (even to help find a word), as it can break the pattern of communication.**
   Allow them the time they need.

7. **Try not to dismiss their worries. Listen and show you are there for them.**

8. **For those with restless hands, a twiddle muff provides a wonderful source of visual, tactile and sensory stimulation. Or create a rummage box, containing objects related to the person's past such as pictures, jewellery or souvenirs, may help as it gives the person an opportunity to move their hands.**

9. **If hallucinations are a common feature of the disease, then offer reassurance, distraction and**

honesty. *For example, if they ask you if you saw it, say, " I know you see something but I don't "*

Affirmation, reassurance, no argument .

Modify the environment if that might help *e.g. lights casting shadows, sounds from TV or equipment…*

o   o   o   o   o   o   o   o   o

Dear Bathing Belle

Tell me, when did this fear of washing begin? Was it as the winter approached or as a new moon arose? Perhaps, it is simply a progression, as surely as night follows day. Whatever the reason, the reluctance has arrived and with it, the stage is set for a whole new range of acting skills. Who is the drama queen now, I wonder – you or I?

How about a shower today? Good. Let me turn up the heating and run the shower in advance, so the room will be lovely and warm for you.

Yes, I know you feel the cold when you have to remove any clothing but you will feel so warm and cosy after you shower. Here we are... just step in.

You no longer want to because it will be cold? Hold your hand under the spray and feel how warm it is. Oh, it is too hot? No, problem...how's that now?

Good, let me help you step in but you do need to take off your nightdress. No, showering with the nightdress on is not an option. Yes, I will leave the room and give you some privacy... just give me a call if you need a hand. Are you in yet?

No, you are thinking about it....Well, don't think too long.

 Hello, that was quick!

Ah, you have not been in...Oh, you have decided to shower tomorrow instead. Mmm, you said that yesterday and all the yesterdays over the past week. How about a bath this evening? Sounds good? Excellent news !

Evening comes and the stage is set for another round of cajoling, negotiating and debate. Do you fancy a bath this evening? No. You would rather have it in the morning. Well, we have been there already and nothing happened. You will be lovely and warm, ready for your bed after a bath. How about it? No. Okay, let's go with tomorrow morning, then.

Here we are again.

I have run your bath. Oh, you are not sure where to go... Well, follow me. Yes, the bath is for you. Add more cold water, then. No, one foot dipped in, albeit briefly, does not constitute bathing. You'll think about it... so, would I please leave the room?

I tell you what, how about you get in and I will rub your back? You are now cold, so you think you will skip it, for today? Yes, I can see that you are thinking of skipping off...

Okay, Ms Motivator is here, so let's exercise in the bathroom, to get warm. One, two, three, four...stretch, turn, bend, up, down...very good! Yes, as you say, this is fun and funny at the same time. Feeling warmer? Good. Right time to get in...

NO, the bath is for you not me. Come on, you really must wash because it is over two weeks since you last bathed and you are beginning to smell. Yes, you do smell but my dear bathing belle, you will smell glorious after your bath, in this sweet smelling water.

I am losing it, both the battle and the will to live!

What can I try next, I wonder?

By this stage, you have adopted that sickly smile, I know only too well and you tell me that you really don't need to listen to me. The "oh, really", "I think not", "you don't say", trips off your tongue in a facetious manner, in response to every sentence that I utter.

God, I am so frustrated, I could scream..Agh!

In triumph, you sail out of the bathroom with a laugh and a look of both utter delight and defiance. The victor retains her position to fight another day.

I get in the bath and drown my sorrows..

Love A

7. Twists and Turns

"There is more to the person than the dementia
(Parliamentary Group)

- The twists and turns of events within this disease certainly require agility and determination.

- See. Hear. Touch. These change and become unrecognisable to someone with dementia. For someone with dementia, 'expectations' (see - hear- touch) are different.

- Claiming items have been stolen is common, e.g. money, possession, keys. Equally, items can be misplaced and found in the strangest of locations.

- Aggressive behaviour, verbal or non verbal may arise for periods – e.g. swearing, biting, slapping are transient behavioural changes that temporarily change the nature of the person. They usually arise when the person does not want to participate and is in a state of anxiety.

- Personal hygiene may become irrelevant to the person, as the fog of dementia descends.

- Refusing to sleep in a bed is common for some people who move into a care home. With time, the inability to walk and to raise their legs when sitting, will result in swelling and other associated physical problems. Buying a comfortable recliner chair that allows them to be raised and semi-flat is a great alternative, to the problem of not using the bed to sleep in.

- Incontinence is part of the dementia disease. While s/he is still aware of their toilet needs they may not understand where the toilet is (regardless of signs) and defecate elsewhere. In time, changing incontinence pads/pants can, in some cases, lead to behavioural challenges – aggression, resistance. With incontinence and lack of mobility, a 'hospital' mattress (wipeable & breathable) and an adjustable bed may keep them more comfortable.

- Teeth cleaning can be a challenge when not fully understanding what is required. Playing a game of rinse and spit can be something of a 'hit and miss' activity. Within a few years of the dementia gaining a hold, attendance at a dentist may be impossible.

- As the journey progresses, hospitalisation may become more common, for a fall or tooth extraction, and with it brings anxiety and misunderstanding.

- Keeping hair clean and trimmed can prove difficult unless a routine is established and a relationship can be formed with the hairdresser. Never give up on trying to set a routine, no matter how hard, It will pay dividends in the long run.

---

1. Don't attempt to reason, just ignore any aggressive remarks/ actions. They are not in control of their behaviours; their damaged brain is.

2. Try to make sense of their world (not yours). Reframe your behaviour.

3. **Agree, don't argue.** *e.g. they say someone has stolen their purse – your response 'I have talked to X and they caught the person, so they won't steal again from you....'*

4. To gain cooperation, approach by –
    - Walking slowly
    - Standing to the side, not in front
    - Getting low, to their height
    - Offering your hand (don't just take theirs)
    - Using their name in a gentle tone
    - Pausing, taking your time
    - Praising. Be sensitive to their feelings.
    - Using music to distract/calm
    - Explaining slowly and simply what you are doing.
    - **Demonstrate what you are about to do** *e.g. gentle brushing of teeth*

5. Caring is not just about the basics of health. It's about bonding and forming relationships with the individual in your care.
    a. What do you know about who they were and are now?
    b. What do you know about their likes and dislikes?

6. **Likes/dislikes will change but there may be some triggers there. A dislike of certain foods becomes more common.** *For example, mixing drink and food on the same plate, whilst a mess, is perfectly acceptable if they 'eat'*

it If they loved golf, bringing a gold ball to feel and touch may produce a 'feel good' factor.

7. **Push the pause button. Find 5 minutes, in the your day, to sit beside them and share time.**
   This is not the sole responsibility of an activity coordinator who may/may not see them once a week. Despite the challenges of staffing in a care home, carer managers build this in to dementia support.
   For example –
   - *look at photographs*
   - *listen to a piece of music*
   - *have a dance (maybe in the chair)*
   - *do a hand or foot massage*
   - *take an item that is tactile and comforting to touch*

   o o o o o o o o o

Hello Mary

You are looking well, come and sit here while Lucy finishes her client's hair. She will be with you shortly and I am going to wash your hair ready for her, to cut and blow dry your hair"

I am so reminded of my own mother, that I feel a mixture of emotions each time I see you. Warmth, love, laughter, tears. You have been coming for quite a few years now and we have seen the changes.. Sadly, previous hairdressers were not so accommodating as your dementia began to affect behaviours but we have a number of elderly clients so we are unfazed by the Alzheimer's maze.

Originally, you would be dropped off and we would get started whilst Alison's quickly nipped to the village shop before retuning. As time progressed, we needed Alison's presence for the whole appointment, either because of your unpredictability, or lack of understanding or mobility issues.

For you, some days are better than others. We have learned over the years, to choose the appointment time carefully. Late mornings and lunchtimes produces the best behaviour, when a quieter salon helps keep you calm. But we have never experienced disruptive or irrational behaviour; simply the loss of speech, mobility and understanding.

Perhaps, the salon is a happy place for you and hence you have not been difficult.. Of course, things will get worse for you but we will continue to support, even in the darkest hour, until the point is reached where Alison cannot manage to bring you.

For now, all is good and for Alison it is a welcome relief to be able to bring you regularly to the salon, which you clearly enjoy, and where she too can relax, enjoy coffee and a chat.

These days Alison lifts you out of the car and holds you, to help you walk the few steps into the salon. On a bad day, the wheelchair is used. Since your hip replacement, your mobility is greatly affected and of course your cognitive abilities continue to decline. But what still remains is your wonderful smile, (albeit these days without the front dentures - it's a bit of a struggle trying to get them in or out) which lights up when you see Lucy. She is definitely your favourite . We don't always understand what you are trying to tell us – language is now a jumble of words - but not to worry, we just go along with it and somehow or other, you are happily engaged in our 'conversation'. Hugs and laughter win the day.

The mirror is both a friend and a foe. Don't we all feel that way when we look at ourselves and see the advancing years…agh, where did those lines come from ! For you, the mirror is mostly a friend. You laugh at yourself or 'your friend' but more often or not, you are focused on Lucy as she chats to you while trimming and drying your hair.

It is difficult to say for sure, how much of our talk you understand but you smile and babble and twinkle. Occasionally, you are disgruntled with the person in the mirror when you simply stare and frown. With Alison's calming influence and Lucy's gentle ways, it is usually a short-lived issue. And you definitely love Lucy, whose charm works wonders for you.

On a good day, while Alison chats or has a short treatment, you are content to sit on the sofa with a magazine which keeps you happily occupied, either looking at the pictures or tearing the pages into strips . Then its all 'hands on deck' to help get you up and out into the car. Happy days.

Let us hope that the fog doesn't roll in too quickly and that you can work your way round the maze, successfully and with little anxiety, for some time to come.

See you next week, Mary

Love Lynn

8. Carers need care too

Looking after someone with dementia can be physically and emotionally draining, often resulting in stress and burnout. To ensure that you can stay the course (for it could be a very long road) the priority is to look after self.

To reduce the stress of caring, try the following –

1. Look after your own health needs by maintaining a healthy diet, taking regular exercise, having friends and/or family to talk with, scheduling time for hobbies, interests, reading, meeting friends...

2. Build in emotional support through dementia support groups, friends, family, neighbours, your line manager if you are a professional carer. Sharing with others who understand what you are going through is supportive and therapeutic.

3. If care is at home, set up some respite. Someone coming in several times a week or a short break with your loved one going into a respite home. If you are a professional carer, make sure that you have a balanced life-work environment allowing for breaks and re-charging of your batteries. Re-charging and

refuelling is important for long term sustainability in caring.

4. if possible, practice meditation techniques to reduce stress – yoga, deep breathing - thereby, reducing anxiety levels and calming the mind.

5. Don't feel guilty at setting boundaries for time off, or refusing additional care duties or asking family members to give you help or a break.

6. If you are a family carer, makes sure that power of attorney is set up to manage all legal and financial affairs, thereby protecting your loved one and reducing the stress on you, as a carer.

7. Get professional help if you are feeling burnt out and cannot cope any longer. Speak to your doctor. Set up an appointment with a therapist, counsellor or other professional support agent.

8. Maintain a positive attitude in order to enjoy time with those you care for and, to concentrate on the good aspects of caring.

o o o o o o o o

9. Lost in Time

"Alzheimer's is just another word for a long goodbye"
(Nancy Reagan)

- **As the dementia advances, the person usually has little or no speech, can no longer move independently and may have lost the ability to maintain their body posture at all. Remember, they are still a loved one throughout this process.**

- **Communication should be there until the end. Never assume that the person cannot hear or understand you.**

- **There is clear evidence – through the power of music, song and touch – that people with advanced dementia do not lose the ability to communicate.**

- **Non-verbal communication is vital. Touch can be used to stimulate senses and provide reassurance. Try to achieve eye contact. Be aware of the tone of your voice and remember that the expression on your face will convey more than the content of your words.**

1. **Do not remind the person if a loved one is dead.** It's not uncommon for people with dementia to believe their deceased spouse, parent or other loved one is still alive. Telling them otherwise can make them upset or angry. BUT if **they ask** if they are dead, then give an honest answer and move on to another topic.

2. **Some people may find touch and human contact reassuring. Sitting with the person, talking to them, brushing their hair and holding hands may help.**

3. **Even though they can't talk, they are still communicating Their eyes are fixed on you and they'll smile and be more relaxed ,when you're doing smiling at them. Read their face. Keep communicating.**

4. **The focus should be on making sure that they are as comfortable as possible. Stimulating the senses can help, for example, with music and aromas that the person likes.**

5. **Take your time and take clues from them. Rushing is the antithesis of confusion and uncertainty.**

Dear Mother and Father

Where are you...? I want to see you.

I have been looking for you on a regular basis. Where are you living now? Have you moved home because I think someone told me you were no longer in Scotland. I think of you all the time and I often speak of you both.

I do appreciate all the things that you have bought me, particularly of late, and know that you must wonder what I am up to, since I haven't been to visit recently. Well, let me tell you...

I am now living in this house where I have my own room. I must just check that all my things are still there...you never know who might steal them. Have you seen my room? Oh, you have...I must have missed you...what a shame! Let me know when you are next coming and I will make sure to be here.

Mother...these are some of my new clothes. I think you bought this pink jumper for me. I have lots of lovely, new things which I am keeping for good.. I know that you rarely wore pretty things but I must confess to liking these pastel colours, pretty earrings and sparkling necklaces.

I suspect you would not approve of my lifestyle. You had few *fineries* in your life and you could be highly critical if you thought I was being vain, immodest or extravagant. You were rarely demonstrative in your affections for me. Of course, perhaps the loss of a daughter, at the age of six, to diphtheria, coloured your outlook. While I never met my sister, I always felt that I could never quite match the tales of her angelic nature. Silly, really... I know that you loved me but it felt to be conditional on meeting your expectations.

Are you coming here, tomorrow..?

Father, I have your watch in my hand. It hung from your waistcoat and you took a pride in winding and polishing it, each evening as you sat by the fireside in the leather armchair. Funny, how I remember this and not other things. Clocks are something I still associate with you... particularly the pendulum clock and the ritual of being allowed to wind up the pulleys. Do you still have that clock?

Are you coming to visit? It will be nice to see you...

Who are you working for now, father? Still, on the croft? Or have you retired?

I remember as a little girl, how I loved you placing me on the horse's back, as you walked it to the plough. I was rather scared but you looked after me well. You were quite soft with the animals and let me keep the lame duck, as my pet. Oh, that duck was funny...following me along the path to the school road and meeting me on my return. Where is she now, I wonder?

I am worried about you.

I think someone told me that you had been ill

Or did they say you were dead?

I wanted to come and see you but I have no way of getting to you and I am not sure if you still live in the same place. I regularly talk of visiting and of coming home to you but somehow it never happens. I would like to be with you.

There are times where I dream about you and wake calling your name. I have even gone looking for you but then that was very silly of me because you live a long, long way away...It is difficult finding my way around this maze.

I do not know where I am.

Where you are.

Dearest mother and father, I miss you.

It will be lovely to see you...

If is too late to come tonight, then perhaps, tomorrow would be better.

I will get up early to meet you.

Where are you?

I will come looking for you....

Love Mary

10.
Time to go

"The meaning of life is that it stops" (Frank Kafka)

- **Early on in the dementia journey, it is important that families have an end of life care plan, before the individual loses cognitive abilities, The dementia sufferer should be encourage to have this discussion, while still able to do so, and to formalise their wishes. Having discussed, planned and recorded their wishes for end of life care, i.e. the treatments, procedures, resuscitation etc., this ensures that their preferences are honoured and treatment is given as needed and desired.**

- **Families should ensure this is detailed in an Advance Care Plan, with the medical and legal professionals. If a person has lost the ability to do this, then their executor who has power of attorney or a healthcare proxy can make decisions on their behalf.**

- In the latter stages of dementia, caring can become more difficult. The physical, medical needs of caring increase. There are special challenges surrounding the end-of-life of someone with dementia, in part because the disease's progression is so unpredictable. Details of caring at this stage are available on many specialist websites. Some are listed at the end of the booklet.

- Palliative care can be given in a hospice, at home or in the care facility. Good care is a collaboration of family and professionals – doctors, nurses, chaplains, social workers.

- Grieving is a normal part of the dying process. Coping with grief and loss is part of the end of life support needed for carers. While knowing that death is imminent, there is still a sense of loss. Talking to others who understand and have experienced loss may help.

- It's easy to assume that when a person is no longer communicating or spending much of their day in bed, the emphasis will be on keeping the person physically comfortable and activities become less relevant. While the person's responses may be more limited (no longer able to move independently

- or hold a conversation), it is important to continue to interact.

  - Even at an advanced of dementia, s/he can still experience emotions - such as loneliness, boredom or frustration - and can respond positively to close one-to-one attention, using the eyes to communicate or hands to touch and make a connection.

  - Work around the senses...
    HEAR...TOUCH...SMELL...TASTE

    ....

1. Always trust that the person has feelings even though facially they may not be able to express them, in the latter stage of life. Make them feel loved and cherished.

2. Try to speak calmly and slowly; be aware of the tone and volume of your voice.

3. Consider sharing familiar stories with the person.

4. Make eye contact, say their name and smile.

5. Use other methods of communication besides speaking, such as gentle touching, stroking hand or forehead or soft toy, or massage hands with cream/oil, press the flat of your hand to theirs, gently giving and resisting in turn.

6. **Be led by any movements/sounds from the person** e.g. a finger dance (responding to the small movement of their index finger), **rather than dominate the communication.**

7. Have the person listen to music or calming nature sounds, such as birdsong or read to them

8. Take time to sit beside them. Focus on the 'here and now' rather than thinking about the next job to be done.

9. Pay close attention to them, making sure you are in their eyeline, so that you don't miss a movement or sound, if they do attempt to communicate something

10. Responses vary from one moment to the next. Never stop trying to engage.

11. Look after yourself. Handling a death is always upsetting. Talk to friends and colleagues and others who have experienced loss and can understand and empathise.

○   ○   ○   ○   ○   ○   ○   ○   ○

Resources for Carers

Local support groups and counselling services can provide opportunities to meet with like minded people. Some offer lunch meetings for carers and their loved ones with dementia

Education and Information is available online through various specialised bodies, such as Alzheimer's Society UK, Alzheimer's Association USA, Dementia UK, Family Caregiver Alliance USA, Marie Curie UK, Alzheimer's Disease International, Carers UK, World Health Organisation, Alzheimer Europe, NCD Alliance, Dementia Alliance International, Dementia Australia, National Institute on Ageing.

Websites:
- www.scie.org.uk/dementia
- www.alz.org/help-support/caregiving
- www.dementiauk.org
- www.mariecurie.org.uk/professionals/palliative-care-knowledge-zone
- www.nia.nih.gov/health/end-life/end-life-care-people-dementia
- www.meaningfulcarematters.com
- www.playlistforlife.org.uk
- https://www.dementia.org.au/resources/alzheimers-disease-international-adi
- https://www.alzint.org/
- https://www.alz.org/global/overview.asp
- https://www.nia.nih.gov/health/alzheimers-causes-and-risk-factors/what-happens-brain-alzheimers-disease

Illustrations

Ron Leishman: under license .
Shutterstock: under license

The Author

Alison was raised in Scotland but now lives in East Anglia with her husband, two dogs and horse. She is a freelance management consultant, with a Doctorate in Business Management and published research on coaching and organizational performance. She cared for her mother, who had dementia, at home for nearly eight years. She is engaged with many friends involved in caring, personally and professionally, for others suffering with various forms of dementia. She is the author *of 'A Scottish Legend in Patagonia'* and *'Laughter and Tears: Journeying through the Alzheimer's Maze'*.

www.ingramcontent.com/pod-product-compliance
Lightning Source LLC
Chambersburg PA
CBHW070628050426
42450CB00011B/3144